FUEL FOR THE BOILER:

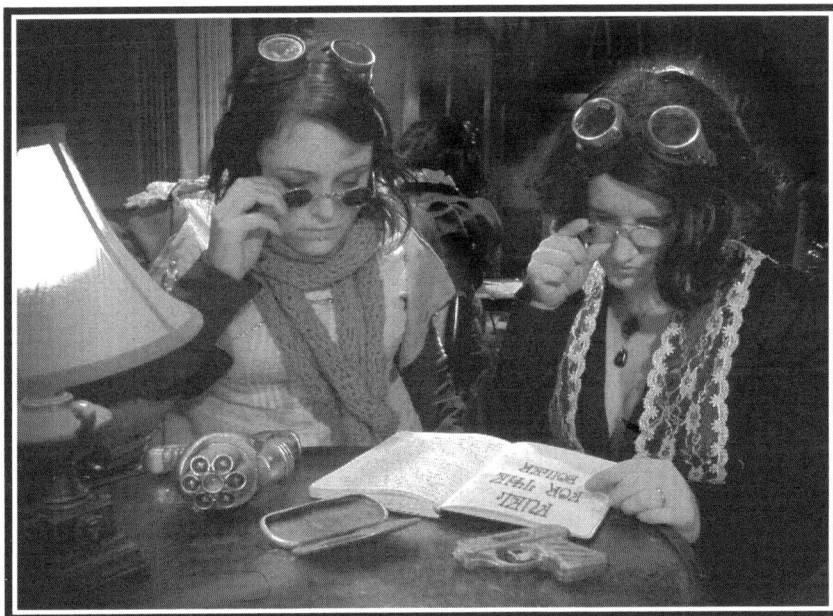

Emmet and Klaude Davenport

A STEAMPUNK COOKBOOK

By Elizabeth Stockton

CONTENT:

INTRODUCTION

Through time there has been one thing that has always held man together. One thing that all humans,and animals for that matter, have in common. Food, food will always be a unifying factor in human kind. Societies have been built upon it, and wars have been fought over it. So, it is little wonder that a group such as our community, would have its own recipe book.

Recipes are not just directions for the creation of a culinary dish. Recipes are, or can be, a form of art. A means to share a heritage or,in the case of this book, a means to bring closer together a small but growing community. When I first proposed this book it was simply an idea to share recipes and print them at home. But after the overwhelming response of all the members of the Brass Goggles forum, I had to make their request a reality. To not only bring together these recipes,but print them for all the world to see and enjoy.

The reader at home maybe wondering what makes this book "steampunk". There are no transistors here,no boilers to explode at inconvenient moments, no sky piracy...well maybe a little of that. But in to-to there really isn't any thing plainly "steamy" And yet, this book is, in my eyes, the very epitomization of steampunk. Steampunk, by its nature,defy definition. It is a group of people,art,literature,and music that lives under an umbrella term. If said umbrella was an undulating concave pillow of brass,steel,steam,and mixed metaphors. This book is similar it is a mix of the works of culinary science of steampunks, and the wit of its authors. And thought my name be on the cover as its author, I am in fact only one of many.

This book has been penned by the many individuals of the steampunk community. The recipes here in have been contributed by members of the community far and wide. As well as images from many steampunks world wide.

I am deeply grateful that I was given this opportunity. This chance to contribute some thing to the wonderful world of fantastical creations and fantastic personalities (and persona). I have labored creating this book,making it a wonder to behold, and I hope I have done so. My hope is that you, gentle reader, will look upon this book and find there is a snap shot of the world of steampunk as it is today.

Ms Boo Dreadful (Elizabeth Stockton)
May 10,1808

DEDICATIONS
&
ACKNOWLEDGMENTS

There are so many people this book is and should be dedicated too. However,i want to dedicate it first and foremost to my husband. If he hadn't been standing next to me telling me I could make this happen... I don't think it would have! Beyond him I want to dedicate this book to Ms Tinkergirl, if it were not for her dedication to the Brass Goggles website and forum, this book really would never have happened! Last, but not least by any means, this book is dedicated to all the brilliant and creative minds of the Steampunk Community.

I would also like to acknowledge all the folk who let me use their images thank you ever so you made this book a visual, as well as culinary journey. Also thank you to all the lovely folk who sent me their recipe, some of which were prized family recipes. Thank you for sharing them with us! To me this was the equivalent of welcoming us into your homes!

And finally I would like to directly thank the crew of the HMS Ophelia for letting me use their images in this book and for being such a wonderful rooting gallery for me! If it were not for the members of the Brass Goggles forum and the crew of the HMS Ophelia rooting me on...i fear I would have lost hope when I had to change printers half way through this project.

A Special thanks goes out to, what I have been calling my "Technical Team" Cap'n Harlock, Ms Cybele 13, and Akumabito these three people helped me hammer out the program as well as spelling, editing, and the like without them I think this book would look like a three year old wrote it!

One last special thank to Mr. SalieriAAX who devised the lovely title of this book you now hold! I would also like to thank Delen, the creator of the book cover!

CHAPTER ONE:

Kristina of the HMS Ophelia

APPETIZERS & BEVERAGES

***

FRUIT HIP FLASK LIQUEURS:

Required Vessel:
Firmly Seal able Jar (Preferably a large French Kilner, but instant coffee jars work just as well)

Ingredients (per 1 liter jar space, measurements are approximate):
550ml clear spirit of your choosing (gin and vodka are recommended)
450g strong-flavored fruit of your choosing (damsons, raspberries, cherries, sloes etc)
300g white caster or granulated sugar

Method:
Empty your chosen spirit into the jar and carefully warm it up to just a little above room temperature (using anything but a naked flame)
Add about 200g of the sugar, firmly close the lid (if you are using a jar with a plastic lid, such as a coffee jar, it is a good idea to line the lid with cling-film) and shake the mixture until all of the sugar has dissolved.
Continue to add the remaining sugar spoonful-by-spoonful until you are certain no more will dissolve or you run out.
If you are using very soft fruit such as Raspberries, Blackberries or Sloes, add them now.
If you are using fruit with a firm skin such as Damsons or Cherries, you will need to prick the skins of each fruit several times before adding them. Hard fruits like Quinces will need to be sliced.
Firmly seal the jar again and put it away in a safe place to mature and infuse, where looters cannot find it.
The ideal timescale for maturation is about six to eight weeks, and remember to check it regularly, shaking it thoroughly if you see sugar crystals on the base.
When the liqueur is infused to your fruity satisfaction (opening the jar while it is infusing won't affect the process, so taste at will), strain and decant into a cut-class decanter or many, many hip flasks.

Waste not want not:
An added delight of making your own liqueurs is that afterwards you are left with a jar of spirit-soaked fruit. There are infinite potential applications for these but my favorites are-
Eton Mess made with gin-soused raspberries.
Devils on Horseback made with alcoholic damsons instead of prunes.

I'm sorry the recipe is so sketchy and ineloquent. I've been making these liqueurs for years, based on my grandmother's method, have never measured out a single ingredient, and have never actually thought about putting the process into words before. I will keep hitting the magic 'modify' key whenever things occur to me to try to make this a bit more elegant.

SalieriAAX

***

PERSONAL MEAD RECIPE

Makes 30 liters

You need:

15 liters of water
15 kilograms of good honey (the better the honey, the better the mead)
3 liters of apple juice
port yeast for 50 liters
a canister of 50 liters, fitted with a fermenting tube
a large funnel
spices of your choice (if you like)
lots of time and patience

Start off by adding the yeast and the apple juice to the container and fitting the fermentation tube. It's a water-based valve. Let it sit in a dark and not too warm place (about 20°C) for about a week. Then you need to mix water and honey. Best results come from a cold mix, which takes time and strength. You need to put it all into a large bucket and knead until it's good. Took me the best part of an hour and strained every single muscle in my hands, but it's worth it. The honey and water go into the container. Add any of your spices of choice (assorted whole pepper works especially fine) and put the fermenting tube back in place. After that, it's at least three months. The longer it sits, the better it gets.

ElShoggotho

***
GINGER ALE

Here's what you'll need:

- 2 to 3 ounces (60 to 90 grams) of fresh ginger root (depending on how strong you like it. You can even add more ginger to this ginger ale recipe)*

- 3 tablespoons of lemon juice

- 3 tablespoons of orange juice

- 3⁄4 cup of sugar (nice to blend white with natural cane sugar if you have it)

- 4 1/2 quarts (5 liters) of water

- Some yeast from the supermarket. Bread yeast will work, but if you happen to have a home brew store around, get a small packet of ale yeast. It's cheap. The lot can be substituted with carbonated water, see below.

- Bottles: see below. This recipe will make eight 16-ounce bottles (approximately 3.6 liters).

 What to do for this ginger ale recipe...

Chop up the ginger root
Simmer the ginger, juices, and sugars in 1½ quart of water for 30 minutes to an hour. The longer you leave it simmer, the stronger it will be.
Remove it from heat and strain it out through a kitchen strainer. Compost the plant material. Mix the brew with the other 3 quarts of water. If using carbonated water, skip the rest and go straight to bottling. Let it all cool till it's lukewarm. On the side in a small jar, stir in 1/8 teaspoon of yeast in with 1⁄4 warm water (not hot!)After 15 minutes, add the yeast solution to your lukewarm brew. Let the brew sit for 10 minutes. Bottle it up!

*Note: Mash or grind the Ginger very fine.

ElShoggotho

**

FAUX ABSINTHE

This is an easy absinthe recipe. I've posted it in the Absinthepunk forum, but I figured I'd mention it here.

Note to purists...don't have kittens! I've had plenty of commercial absinthe from all over and this stuff holds up to it extremely well!

First, you make a wormwood infusion:
Soak 1/3 cup dried wormwood in a fifth of 100-proof vodka. Store in a cool, dark place for two weeks.
Strain the infusion into another bottle using a funnel and a coffee filter. Be patient, this takes time.

Next, you buy a bottle of Pernod. Add 1/4 cup to 1/3 cup infusion to the bottle.
(Do not go over this amount...it becomes undrinkable)
At this point, I sweeten the mix with honey. The absinthe ritual is fun, but for anyone who's tried it, sugar doesn't dissolve so well, even if it's set on fire.

Lastly, pour yourself a shot, top it with cold water, and enjoy. This version yields a milder absinthe with a lower alcohol content. The effects come best after sipping a couple glasses slowly over the course of a few hours.

And for the love of all that is holy, please, do not take shots of the pure tincture! Your stomach will hate you, if the shot even passes your gag reflex.

For something closer to true absinthe in alcohol content, Absente can be used instead of Pernod. While it contains Roman wormwood (not so strong in thujone), the infusion gives it the right amount of kick.

Rose Streiffe

***

SAUTÉED SEA SCALLOPS ON ASPARAGUS RAFTS WITH ORANGE MARMALADE, A LA CYBELE

Large sea scallops, two or three per serving
Wondra or other light flour to coat the scallops
thin asparagus spears, cut to uniform lengths - roughly three inches, depending on the size of the scallops - you'll need six per raft
Three or four slices of bacon, cooked crispy and crumbled
Two or three oranges to juice (or roughly 1 cup/8 fl. oz. of OJ)
1/2 cup chicken stock, with a little left over, just in case you need it
1 small shallot, minced
1/2 garlic clove, minced
Clarified butter or flavorful oil, such as an Italian or Spanish olive oil
salt and pepper to taste

Juice the oranges, getting enough juice for 1 cup or 8 fluid ounces.

In roughly 1/2 Tablespoon of clarified butter or oil, saute the shallot until soft and translucent. Add garlic. Saute one or two minutes. Slowly pour in orange juice, lower heat, and cook down. The OJ will begin to thicken. Add the chicken stock, a little at a time, to keep the OJ mixture thick, but liquid enough to "glop" off a spoon, much like warmed jelly. Taste periodically and salt and pepper as desired. This will NOT be a sweet marmalade.

While you're cooking the OJ, bring a pot of salted water to a boil in order to blanch the asparagus. Place asparagus in boiling water long enough for them to maintain their bright green color and some of their natural "snap," roughly 60 seconds, probably less if you have really thin ones.

Remove asparagus from the water and immerse in ice water to stop them from cooking further, but remove them before they cool too much. They don't have to be hot when served, but warm is nice.

Clean scallops, salt and pepper them, dredge in Wondra. Heat saute pan with butter or oil to just below the smoke point. Shake excess flour from scallops and carefully place them in saute pan. Saute on each side until a deep golden color on each side. The flour will prevent them from becoming too moist as they cook and should create a nice, almost crunchy coating.

To assemble: To create a "raft" of asparagus, place three spears on the plate next to each other, evenly spaced. Take another three spears and place them crosswise on top of the first three. Take a cooked scallop and carefully place it on the "raft." Spoon a bit of the marmalade on the top of the scallop and sprinkle with some of the bacon crumbles.

Two or three of these rafts can serve as a full appetizer for one person.

*Note: I have been told these are tasty. Though I developed the idea and cooked them, I have never tasted them as I am allergic to shellfish.

Cybele13

***

EGGNOG

4 egg yolks
1/3 cup sugar, plus 1 tablespoon
1 pint whole milk
1 cup heavy cream
3 ounces bourbon
1 teaspoon freshly grated nutmeg
4 egg whites
In the bowl of a stand mixer, beat the egg yolks until they lighten in color. Gradually add the 1/3 cup sugar and continue to beat until the sugar completely dissolves. Add the milk, cream, bourbon and nutmeg and whisk to combine.
Place the egg whites in a different bowl of a stand mixer and beat to soft peaks using the whisk attachment. With the mixer still running gradually add the 1 tablespoon of sugar and beat until stiff peaks form.
Whisk the egg whites into the mixture. Chill and serve.
Makes 6 to 7 cups.

Steven S.

***

RHUBARB WINE

Sterilize a bucket
Cut a kilo or two of rhubarb stems into chunks, freeze overnight, place in bucket
pour on some water ~5L
mash rhubarb a bit with a blunt object
put a cloth over the bucket to keep flies out
leave for a couple of weeks-until the mold is a couple of inches thick
scoop off mold and filter the juice into a sterilized demijohn with 1.5 kg of sugar
Add some grape juice if you want
Add a sachet of wine yeast-follow the instructions
top the demijohn off with water
leave it in a cool place say 18 deg centigrade with an airlock in the jar
when bubbling activity ceases, siphon the wine off the dead yeast sludge into a
clean demijohn. Leave for 8 to 12 months and bottle

Dauntless

***

DARKRAVEN'S TACO DIP

Ingredients:
1 can of frozen avocado dip or fresh mashed avocado
1 cup of sour cream you an use fat free/low fat
½ cup of mayonnaise again low fat/fat free
1 package taco seasoning low sodium <-- important
1 or 2 cans of refried beans if you use the fat free you can not tell
1 large bunch of green onions with tops, chopped
1 medium size plum tomato, cored, sliced and seeded
1 small can pitted black olives, chopped
1 8 oz package sharp cheddar cheese, shredded can use low fat
Combine avocado, sour cream, mayonnaise and taco seasoning in a bowl.
To assemble dip; spread beans in a medium sized, shallow serving platter. Top
with avocado mixture. Sprinkle with chopped onions, tomatoes, and black olives.
Cover with the cheese. Serve chilled or at room temperature

What I changed - I hate avocados, so I mixed the taco seasoning into the sour cream instead. It wasn't as pretty but it tasted great. I used fat free refried beans and mayo and reduced fat cheese, sour cream, and tortilla chips with no complaint. My father in law hates all things healthy and he ate most of this. I also added diced jalapeños to the beans.

Lily

***

CHEESY GOO OR DIGBY'S SAVORY TOASTED CHEESE

3 parts cream cheese

2 parts butter

1 part brie (remove rind)

Melt cream cheese, butter, and, brei together. Whip with hand beater. Dip bread, vegetables, etc into it while warm. Keeps nicely in a fondue pot.

Hexidecima

***

MEAD RECIPE

Ingredients:
1 Gallon Water
Honey, 5 Lb. for Sweet, 4 for dryish
1 in. Cinnamon Stick
Zest and juice from 1 lemon
Tea bag
Champagne yeast

FUEL FOR THE BOILER

Equipment:
4 liter wine jug empty
1 gallon jug, empty
Vapor lock (also known as a fermentation lock) w/ rubber stopper with hole in the center ("the bubbler")
Funnel
Clear plastic tubing (food grade)
Cork + whatever type of bottles you intend to store it in when it's done.

While bringing water to a good roiling boil:
Add tea bag, use your favorite herbed/spiced tea. Note this is to provide the tannin, so be sure it has some real tea in it. I use always use Vanilla Almond tea from The Republic of Tea and sometimes add Constant Comment from Bigelow and/ or Chai Spice tea from Stash
Add lemon zest, lemon juice, cinnamon stick
Remove tea bag (s) when brew is a light amber…really weak tea.
Add honey once water is boiling…keep the jars of honey in a warm place (like a pan of hot water) so it's easier to pour. Save one of the jars and a lid.
When the pot returns to boil, begin skimming off the foam. Yeah, this removes the zest, that's why we put it in early.
When you are sick and tired of skimming, and have most if not all the foam gone, and the thing has been boiling for around 45 minutes or more, turn off the heat and cover and let cool.
When the proto-mead is down to around 95 Degrees F. dip out about 1/4 cup and dissolve yeast into it.

Clean the larger wine jug out really really well. Rinse thoroughly with lots o' hot water. And let cool

Put the big jar in the sink, in case you spill. Using the funnel, pour the yeast mixture into the jug. Then pour in the proto-mead, only filling to the bottom of the neck.

If you use 5 lb. of honey you will probably have some proto-mead remaining. If making sweet mead, pour it into one of the empty honey jars, put on the lid and put it into the fridge. You'll use it later. If trying for a dryer mead you can discard the remaining proto- mead.

Fill the bubbler/ airlock about 1/2 full of water.

You should start to see the bubbles shortly. The better you mixed the yeast the longer it takes to start bubbling, but that's a good thing. Too active too soon and it will foam into the bubbler. If that does happen, just rinse out the bubbler and put it back on.

For the first 12 days shake the mead daily. Doesn't have to be a lot of shaking, just enough to wake up the yeasties and get them going. Let it sit quietly for 2 more days

FIRST DECANTING:

The Splash

Clean the gallon jug very well. Siphon the mead into the gallon jug, allowing it to splash onto the bottom. Siphon off as much as you can, try not to disturb the residue at the bottom. You should be able to get a gallon out of it easy enough. Replace the bubbler and let the mead sit quietly for a week. Wash the 4 liter jug out very well.

SECOND DECANTING:

Siphon the mead into the wine jug, no splashing this time, let it run down the inside of the jug. Once again, leave the residue. Transferring from the gallon to the wine jug will leave the jug not quite full. If making sweet mead use the remaining proto- mead from the fridge. If making dryer mead, use water to top off to the neck.
Let sit quietly for another week.

THIRD DECANTING:

From the 4 liter jug to the gallon jug. Let sit quietly another week.

Continue alternating until the mead clears. Once clear, the alcohol content should be around 12%, a goodly wine. A hygrometer will give you an exact reading. The percent alcohol is a factor of how much honey is dissolved, so you need to take a reading before fermentation. Bottle as you will. Make sure it's done fermenting or there is the distinct possibility that your bottles may burst if tightly sealed. To stabilize the mead for long periods, you may add a crushed Campden tablet, these contain sulfates and act as preservatives. If you use one it should be added at the 3rd decanting. These tablets are found in the same stores that you can find the yeast and the fermentation locks.

hexidecima

***

FRIED KRAKEN (SQUID)

Vegetable oil, for deep-frying
1 pound clean squid with tentacles, bodies cut into 1/3- to 1/2-inch-thick rings
2 cups all-purpose flour
2 tablespoons dried parsley
Salt and freshly ground black pepper

Pour enough oil into a heavy large saucepan to reach the depth of 3 inches. Heat over medium heat to 350 degrees F. Mix the flour, parsley, salt, and pepper in a large bowl. Working in small batches, toss the squid into the flour mixture to coat. Carefully add the squid to the oil and fry until crisp and very pale golden, about 1 minute per batch. Using tongs or a slotted spoon, transfer the fried calamari to a paper-towel lined plate to drain.
I a few chopped jalapeños thrown in for a bit of spice.

Franklin Wrayburn

CHAPTER: TWO

Doctor When, Jon , Otta Spaceman, Herr Döktor, Ivan Drugostov,
Rosel, and Tinkergirl

MAIN DISHES

***

SHEPARD'S PIE

I grew up eating this stuff and its one of the greatest things you can do with some leftovers.

Size really depends on how many you are feeding. Since this tends to be used to use up some left overs from a large dinner I am approximating quantities.

6 med potatoes (you can also substitute dried mash potatoes)
1lb Hamburger (I would suggest 90% fat free)
2 cans cream corn
Couple pats of butter

Peel the potatoes and boil them till you can turn them into mashed potatoes. Cook you hamburger in a skillet till it is browned. Drain the fat.

Now get a 9x13 baking pan. Layer in the hamburger then the creamed corn and top with the mashed potatoes. Place a few pats of butter on top of the potatoes.

Preheat your oven to 350 degrees F. Once pre-heated place the baking sheet in the over for about 30 minutes. Once the potatoes are golden to a light brown on top you know its done. Remove from oven and serve.

It has been a while since I last made this so the quantity of potatoes might be a little off.

By Dr. Veleck Madlove

***

TARTE FLAMBÉE.

You need:
Utensils:
a large bowl
a smaller bowl
a baking tray, ideally a round one for pizza

for the dough:
500 grams / roughly 1 pound of wheat flour
half a standard cube (22 grams) of yeast
150 ml each of fresh milk and light beer
Sugar and salt

for the topping:
150 grams of diced ham
250 grams of crème fraîche, can be substituted with thick sour cream
a large onion
salt, pepper and assorted seasonings

The dough has to be prepared some time beforehand. For the starter, you take the yeast and mix it with just a pinch or two of flour, some water and some sugar. It has to be mixed really well in a larger jar, it needs room to rise. Let it do so for at least half an hour. At the same time, take the remaining flour and mix it with the salt. It has to be in the flour itself, salt is poison for yeast when given pure. After the starter has risen, mix it into the flour. Add milk and beer and knead the lot for a few minutes. It has to feel smooth. Add pinches of milk and beer if needed. Let the dough rise for another half hour.
Meanwhile, fry the onions in some butter. Not too much. Mix the fried onions with the cream, add a bit of salt and some more pepper. Personally, I like to add a pinch of cumin, traditionally it should be a pinch of nutmeg.
Put the dough on a floured baking tray, roll it out. Flour the dough along the way. If there's too much dough, you can take aside the excess and make some excellent buns from it.
Anyway, you can add the topping now. Spread the cream and onion mix on the dough, put the diced ham on top of it. The whole lot goes into a pre-heated oven at full steam. Electrical ovens should be set to 250°C/480°F, gas and ventilated ovens can be set to 200°C/390°F. Leave it in there for about 15 to 20 minutes, until the dough is golden brown.
Serve it with a good ale.
ElShoggotho

***

FRANKENCHICKEN -
BUTTERFLIED ROAST CHICKEN WITH CHORIZO STUFFING

1 roaster chicken (approx. 3 lbs)

- Stuffing
2 links fresh chorizo sausage
1 medium-to-large onion
.5 lb fresh crimini (or other) mushrooms
approx 1 tbsp. chopped garlic
one half loaf day-old bread (baguette)
chopped fresh (flat-leaf) parsley
1-2 eggs

-- Stock
3 onions
3 stalks celery
3-4 large carrots
garlic to taste
about a dozen peppercorns
fresh parsley
fresh thyme
bay leaf
water to cover

begin by preparing the chicken - it sounds harder than it actually is.

----CHICKEN AND STOCK PREP----

  Cut off both wings. Toss directly into stockpot. there's not enough meat on the wings to even worry about.
  "Snap" the thigh joints out to their sockets, just like you normally would when cutting up a chicken.
 Using either a cleaver or a pair of kitchen shears, cut along either side of the backbone, and remove it. Add to stockpot.
 With a cleaver or heavy knife blade, cut through the thighbone, right above the "knob" at the lower end (This makes it easier to remove thighbone)
 Dis articulate the thigh/hip joint. Cut around the meat at the top of the bone,

and scrape down the bone with your boning knife, and just pull the entire bone out,

leaving a "hollow" thigh. Repeat on other side.

Loosen breasts from rib bones, with boning knife. When only keel bone is attached

to skin, just yank and the whole bone structure will come loose, leaving skin and meat

with no bones.

Toss all bones into stock pot, and turn up heat - brown the bones a bit - it makes a BIG difference in the final flavor of the stock.

when browned, add rough-cut veggies, herbs and add water to cover. Bring to a boil,

then lower to a simmer. Prep the onion for the stuffing and toss skin and root in as well.

wrap chicken and refrigerate, while your stock simmers for an hour or so. (if you add

extra fresh thyme and garlic, you will end up making a chicken soup-base that can

raise the dead, much less cure colds. Your grandmother was right....)

----STUFFING ----

grind up the bread in food processor (or just wimp out and use store-bought).
skin, chop up and brown the chorizo sausage. Add to bowl.
lightly brown onion and garlic in the rendered chorizo grease. Add to bowl.
brown the chopped mushrooms and add to the mix.
add the breadcrumbs and mix.
add some of the stock, until it's moist but not too squishy. Taste for salt
and pepper now - the chorizo can be VERY salty, so you may not need to add any.
While stuffing cools, get out the chicken, and strain and de-fat the stock.
When stuffing has cooled, add in the egg to bind the stuffing.

----FRANKENCHICKEN----

Put on your white mad-scientist lab coat.
using cotton kitchen twine (NOT nylon, polyester, etc.), tie up the open
ends of the chicken thighs (or else your stuffing will all fall out the end...)
find your reading-glasses, and thread a trussing needle with more string.
(you can get a "real" trussing needle at kitchen store, but they are a royal
pain.. go to a discount store with a fabric section and but a "Craft Needle

Assortment" for about a buck. Use any of the long, large-eyed needles.)
IF stuffing is not extremely salty, season inside of laid-open chicken with
salt and pepper (remember tasting the stuffing?)
 Sprinkle a layer of chopped parsley over the inside of the chicken and inside
the openings where the thighbones used to live.
 push the (cooled) stuffing into the thighbone openings first, then cover the
inside of the chicken.

 Using the needle, make a few "baseball-stitches" to close up bottom of the
chicken, between the thighs. if the skin tears easily, go through a little of
the meat - You'll need to "re-shape" the bird.

 continue up the center, closing up the entire bird, and making it vaguely
 chicken shaped. (if you are in a VERY odd mood - make 2, and stitch them
together,
 neck-end to neck-end - guests will have no idea what it is - mention "nuclear
power
 plant", in passing.....)

 Rub the skin lightly with olive oil, salt and pepper (and I like to sprinkle
 lightly with hot Hungarian paprika, or Cajun spice blend)

 Roast on a rack at 350-375 degrees. (about 1 hr, 15 min, in my oven - internal
temp of
 145 degrees is the target. The butterflied chicken cooks much faster than a
bone-in bird.)
 A very small amount of water added to pan will keep drippings from burning.

 When done, remove and let the meat rest at least 10 minutes. Deglaze the
roasting pan with some of your stock and reduce. Thicken if desired.

 When meat has rested, cut and remove the string (it's tasty, but a terrible
consistency....). To serve, just use a long serrated bread-knife to slice across
it in approx. 3/4" slices (think "meatloaf-style" - no bones to carve around).
White-meat fans get front-end slices, dark-meat lovers get beck-end slices.

--- SERVING SUGGESTIONS ---

Try it with a turkey and your favorite turkey stuffing for the most moist
Thanksgiving Day meal of your life.
Fill the bottom of the roasting pan with sliced red or Yukon-Gold potatoes.
A warmed slice of the leftovers with a spring-green salad and mango-
salsa.CapnHarlock

***

RUBBER MALLET "SPANAKOPITA" CHICKEN

skinned and boned chicken thighs (Breasts would work too, but thighs are cheap and tasty)
1 pkg. frozen spinach, thawed and squeezed dry
crumbled feta cheese (if you don't like feta - use your imagination- provolone? Gorgonzola? cheddar?)
buttermilk (yeah, it DOES have a use)
2 cups Corn Chex<tm> or equivalent (approximate)
salt
black pepper
cumin
oregano (fresh or dried))
cayenne pepper
<optional - cayenne pepper-type hot sauce (Texas Pete / Crystal, etc.)>
pre-mixed Greek seasoning mix (Cavendish or other)

*PLEASE NOTE: I never measure anything!**

 Bone and skin package of chicken thighs (Make stock !!!!) (A pro boning knife costs $40. a sharpening
   stone costs $10. A crappy boning knife costs $1 at a dollar store. Do the math and learn to sharpen.)
 Pound the chicken slightly between 2 layers of plastic wrap - you aren't making scallopini -
   just even out the thickness - (lose the metal hammer with teeth as anything but a REALLY kinky sex toy
   - get a rubber mallet for $3 in the automotive or camping section at WalMart)
 Marinate chicken in fridge for a few hours in buttermilk, salt, black pepper, cayenne,
   cumin and Greek seasoning mix. (hot sauce helps too.) The buttermilk will flavor and tenderize
   the chicken, and at as "glue" to hold the breading.
 Thaw frozen spinach, squeeze all excess water out (into the stock you're cooking - remember that??)
 Mix spinach, some salt, black pepper, oregano, crumbled feta cheese and a little Greek seasoning mix.
 Put corn chex into a plastic bag and beat the crap outta them with any available blunt heavy object.

(another use for that rubber mallet). Aim for "breadcrumb" consistency.
 Wipe inside (not skin side) of each pounded thigh, add a fat tablespoon of spinach/cheese mix,
   fold over and use toothpicks/skewers to close up the package.
 Roll chicken packages in the crumbled cereal until covered/breaded
 Place on a cookie sheet (cover w/foil - I hate cleaning dishes)
 Drizzle with a bit of olive oil to help browning.
 Put chicken in 400 degree oven for about 35 min - until golden brown. (watch the stuff, fer chrissakes.
   - no 2 ovens are the same - might take 25, might take 45)
 wrap in foil and let 'em sit 5 minutes.

CapnHarlock

***

A DASHING DISH OR THE CHICKEN CREATURETORRI

Great-Granddad gave me a pearl-handled pocket-knife and informed me that a gentleman ought to be able to prepare a light supper in twenty minutes without removing his shirt-cuffs. This is as yet my best answer -- a hot dinner for two that requires nothing special but has some flair, and is produced all of a sudden.

1 chicken breast
garlic
olive oil
(somewhere about) 2 tablespoons dried oregano
(somewhere about) 3 tablespoons dried basil
garlic
1 tomato of ordinary, tennis-ballish size
1/2 green bell pepper (or just one, if you can get the smaller ones)
dry pasta of your choice
grated hard nutty cheese of your liking, Parmesan, Asiago, Romano and the like

Cut the chicken into bite-sized pieces and cook them in a large skillet with about half a centimeter of olive-oil in the bottom. Slice in several cloves of garlic, in thin discs. I usually do four or five.

As it's cooking, start the water to boil for pasta and start to chop the tomato. Do not attempt to de-seed it, and try to keep all of the juice that spills out as you chop. Core and de-seed the pepper and slice it lengthwise to produce thin C-shaped strips. Watch the chicken as you go. When it is nearly fully cooked, add the dried herbs to it and give it a stir. Turn down the heat, cover it and start the pasta cooking. When the pasta is about four minutes from being perfectly cooked, put the vegetables (and rescued drops of tomato juice) in with the chicken, stir it up and cover it again. By the time the pasta is finished, drained and put in bowls, the pepper should be hot but still crisp. Spoon the chicken-tomato-pepper stuff over the pasta, and every drop of liquid you can scrape from the pan. Diners spoon copious amounts of the grated cheese over their servings and stir, getting noodles coated in flavored olive-oil and peppered with the cheese and oil-soaked dried herbs.

Mushrooms are a good addition. It looks very pretty if you use yellow and red as well as green pepper.

Ben Franklin's Electric Kite

***

BEGGAR'S CHICKEN WITH CANTONESE MIXED PICKLES

FIRST, CANTONESE MIXED PICKLES.

For that one, we need:
one cucumber
one carrot
some ginger
a quarter pound of Chinese cabbage
a fresh chili pod (larger variant)
Two tea spoons of sugar
one and a half tea spoons each of salt and vinegar

27

Wash and chop the vegetables, put them into a bowl and add salt and vinegar. Mix thoroughly, cover the bowl and let it sit for six hours. Wash the vegetables again, add sugar and put the lot into the refrigerator (or hang it outside the cabin when flying high). Leave it there for another six hours, or until you need it.

SECOND, BEGGAR'S CHICKEN

We need:
one whole chicken, cleaned and ready for the oven
200 grams of pork
50 grams of Cantonese mixed pickles
100 grams of fresh soy beans (alternatively standard white beans)
120 grams of bamboo shoots
some morels (about five)
lotus leaves (about four)
some leaves of Chinese cabbage (about six)
an egg
half a table spoon of starch
light soy sauce
shaoxing wine

some rose wine (玫瑰露酒)

roasted sesame oil

Sichuan pepper

salt

monosodium glutamate (optional, but recommended)

three kilograms of non-poisonous clean clay (alternatively a tight-fitting Italian

clay pot)

some flour

Wash the chicken and pierce the skin in multiple places. Marinate in a mixture of salt, sesame oil and rose wine for about an hour. Chop the pork and marinate it in a mixture of starch, MSG, salt and sichuan pepper. Finely cut the pickles and the morels.

Stir-fry the pork, pickles, morels and soy beans. Add soy sauce, shaoxing wine and MSG as you see fit. Cook the chicken in salt water for about ten minutes. After that, fill it with the stir-fry mix. Sew the opening shut, tie wings and legs to the body with a heat-tolerant thread. Wrap the lotus leaves around it and model a layer of clay around the whole thing. Put it in a pre-heated oven at 230°C (about 450°F) for about two hours, after that turn the temperature down to 120°C (about 250°F). With the Italian pot, it takes two and a half hours at 200°C (about 390°F). To top it off, it should be opened directly at the table with chisel and wooden hammer.

Rice or mie noodles go well with it. The remaining 玫瑰露酒 can be used as a digestion aid. As a normal beverage, I'd serve a dry white wine.

*Note:
Savoy cabbage works as a substitute for lotus leaves.
Excess filling can be served as a side dish, the stir-fry is enough to make it great.
In fact, the filling can be used as a main dish if in a hurry.
The rose spirit is sold as "Mei Kuei Lu Chiew" in most Chinese food stores.
Heavy stuff, don't use too much! American value would be around 110 proof, Imperial value is less than 100. 54 percent of volume is alcohol.****

ElShoggotho

***

OZARK DUBLIN CODDLE

1lb/ 500g Summer Sausage

FUEL FOR THE BOILER

8oz/ 250g Fatty Bacon, Thick cut is best.
1/2pt/ 300ml/ 1 cup Beef Stock
6 medium potatoes
2 medium onions
1 Head Cabbage
salt and pepper
(serves four)

Cut the bacon into 1in/ 3cm squares. Fried up said bacon then bring the stock to the boil in a medium saucepan which has a well-fitting lid, add the sausages and the bacon and simmer for about 5 minutes. Remove the sausages and bacon and save the liquid. Cut each sausage into four or five pieces. If you are using one long piece of sausage cut it into bite size pieces. Peel the potatoes and cut into thick slices. Skin the onions and slice them. Cut the cabbage into wedges. Assemble a layer of potatoes in the saucepan, followed by a layer of onions , a layer of cabbage and then half the sausages and bacon. Repeat the process once more and then finish off with a layer of potatoes. Pour the reserved stock over and season lightly to taste. Cover and simmer gently for about an hour. Adjust the seasoning and serve piping hot.

Ms Boo Dreadful E.V.S.

***

CORNED BEEF A LA HARLOCK

This experiment turned out INSANELY good - I had to share :

2lb package uncooked corned beef brisket (with spice packet from grocery store - don't remove the fat)
3 medium yellow onions, sliced
2 carrots, large chunks
2 stalks celery, large chunks
approx 1.5 tbsp chopped garlic
1tsp mustard seed, whole
1tsp coriander seed, whole
1 tsp black peppercorns, whole
.5 tsp allspice
(note lack of added salt)

FUEL FOR THE BOILER

Rinse the vacuum-packed corned beef under running water for a few minutes. While it rinses (SALT FROM HELL!!!!), sauté onions, carrots, celery and garlic in olive oil. When the veg softens, add the spice packet and spices and cook a few minutes. (spice packet = same spices listed + juniper berries.. it can use more)

Remove veggies and reserve. Dry the corned beef and sear all sides in hot pan with a bit of oil.

Lay out 2 sheets of aluminum foil at 90degrees to each other. Put 1/2 of the veggies on the foil. place the seared brisket on top, and cover with the remaining veg. Seal the foil tightly around the food, then seal second layer. If you're paranoid, use 3 layers of foil.

Put the foil packet into a 250degree F. oven, with a sheet pan/cookie sheet on the rack below, to catch drips, just in case. Don't bother preheating oven.

Walk away and let it cook for 8-10 hours, really - just walk away. Think BBQ.

After 10 hours, or when the smell is just too good to resist, remove the packet, put it over a heatproof container, such as a Pyrex measuring cup, and stab the foil to let it drain. Unlike other oven braises, the liquid is GHASTLY - Salty, nasty and fat-laden. Feel free to toss it without remorse.

Cool meat and refrigerate overnight. Shred while warm if you want corned-beef hash, leave whole and slice for sandwiches.

AMAZING!!

CapnHarlock

***

COLONIAL CURRY

(serves 4)

The usual caveat applies here: this is my own recipe and I don't usually measure the ingredients. I tried to convert them as well as possible
but it won't be 100 % accurate. Variation and experimentation with the recipe are therefore welcomed and encouraged.

You'll need:

- around 450 g of your preferred meat (chicken and lamb are the most traditional but any meat should work)
- around 150 ml of plain yogurt
- a generous amount (at least 4 tablespoons, more if you want) of good garam masala or preferred curry powder (some purists insist on mixing their own spices but I find that getting really good curry powder from an Indian store is easier and more "authentic". It also saves you a lot of additional work.)
- 3 garlic cloves
- a bit of fresh ginger root, about 1 cm in length
- salt
- ghee or butter, alternatively oil
- 2 medium to large onions
- 3 to 4 chillies, cut into rings (depending on how hot you want the curry to become you can remove the seeds.)
- more garam masala to taste

Dice the meat roughly. Peel the ginger root and garlic, dice them finely and (if available) crush them with a mortar and pestle.
Mix the meat with the yogurt, garlic, ginger, curry powder and half a teaspoon of salt in a large bowl. (At this point I also like to add a bit of cumin. This isn't necessary, though and some people don't like the taste).
Cover and let marinate for at least one hour. Chop the onion roughly and fry it in a wok (or large pan) until soft and light brown. Add the marinated meat, fry until brown, cover and let cook over light heat for around 40 minutes. Add chillies halfway through. Stir in more curry powder to taste.
Serve with Basmati rice.

Note: You may have noticed that I overuse the word "roughly". I firmly believe

32

that in home cooked meals, especially in those that are stewed, the main ingredients shouldn't be chopped up too finely.
Don't dice the onion finely, eighths are fine. The cubes of meat shouldn't be too small either. Your meal might take longer to cook but it will be more flavorful, juicier and look better!

Buford Mathias, Esq. FRS

***

MEAT PIES RECIPE

FLAKY CHEDDAR CHEESE CRUST

(courtesy of Rose Beranbaum's Pie and Pastry Bible. Wonderful book. Get it if you like to cook.)

The following makes a 9" single crust. I usually make a double batch and get about a dozen hand-pies from it

8 Tbsp butter (don't use anything else)

1 ½ c. white flour

¼ tsp. salt (don't use if you use salted butter)

1/8 tsp baking powder

¼ tsp. cayenne pepper (can omit or add extra)

¾ c. sharp cheddar cheese, grated and cold

2 ½ Tbsp ice water

1 ½ tsp. cider vinegar

Cut the butter into small cubes (3/4 inch) and wrap in plastic wrap and refrigerate at least 30 minutes.

Place flour, salt, baking powder and cayenne in a gallon zip lock bag. Add cheddar cheese. Seal the bag, pressing most of the air out. Rub cheese and flour mixture together until it resembles a coarse meal. Open bag and add butter cube. Close bag and expel the air. Once sealed, use a rolling pin or flatten the butter into thin flakes. Place bag into freezer for 10 minutes or until butter flakes are very firm.

Open bag. Scrap sides of bag with a spatula to get butter flakes and flour into bottom of bag. Add ice water and vinegar. Seal bag, expelling most of the air. Knead the mixture in the bag until mixture holds together in one piece and feels slightly stretchy when pulled. Take the dough out of bag, flatten into a disc and wrap in plastic or just replace in bag and seal. Refrigerate at least 45 minutes, preferably overnight.

Take out of refrigerator and let set 5-10 minutes so dough is workable. Cut or tear dough into walnut sized hunks. Roll out between wax paper until 1/8" or so thick, usually about 7" diameter roughly. Fill with cooled filling, by placing a tablespoonful or so on half of the circle leaving a margin of about ½". Moisten margin and fold over rest of dough, pressing to seal. Make a small slit on top to release steam.

TO MAKE THE BEEF FILLING:

Take a 3-5 pound beef chuck roast
Envelope of onion soup mix plus 1 cup water
3 cups water
thickener of milk or water and cornstarch or flour

Chuck is what you want, even if some other cut is cheaper. It has enough fat to make the filling tender and juicy. Place the chuck roast in a roasting pan, the type that your grandmother had with the lid. Mix envelope of onion soup mix with a cup of water and pour over roast. Add 3 more cups of water. Preheat your oven to 450 degrees. Place roast pan in oven then reduce the oven temperature to 350 degrees. Roast until you can easily pull apart with a fork, about 2 to 3 hours. Add water if it gets low. You want about 3 cups of meat juices when you're done. When done, remove roast from pan. Dissect roast and remove all chunks of fat and gristle, and tear the meat into shreds. Take meat juices and pour into saucepan. Make a thickener of a loose paste of water/milk and cornstarch or flour. Bring juices to the boil and add thickener by the tablespoonful until it thickens to a good gravy. Cool gravy. Add to meat until it makes a moist mixture. You don't want too much gravy. Cool mixture. And proceed as above.

The pies can sit for a day before baking, but make sure to refrigerate. To bake hand-pies:

Preheat oven to 400 degrees.   Place pies on cookie sheet or jelly roll pan. Bake for 20-30 minutes. They will usually leak a bit of gravy but that doesn't hurt anything.

That's it! These are very good with horseradish sauce or the extra gravy and a beer

hexidecima

***

GRILLED TOMATO, MOZZARELLA, AND BASIL SANDWICH

1 loaf Foccacia Bread
2-3 Large Fresh Tomatoes,sliced
1 Package Fresh Mozzarella(the good stuff folks),sliced thin
1/4 cup Calamata Olives
1/4 cup Basil Pesto
3-4 T Extra Virgin Olive Oil
1 clove garlic
1 bunch of baby spinach greens
an Out Doors Grill

Slice the loaf of bread in half horizontally. While you slice every thing else,place the bread cut side up, under your broiler for just a handful of seconds. While that is toasting mix your olives and pesto,and 1 tablespoon of olive oil in a bowl. Remove the toast from the oven and rub the garlic clove on the toasted side of each piece, liberally. Now begin layering your ingredients, a layer of cheese,then tomato,then spoon on the olive pesto mix,then spinach greens. Start again ending with a layer of cheese. Place the top piece of bread on the bottom and take it to the grill!Paint on a nice layer of Olive Oil, as though it where BBQ sauce and,grill both sides until the cheese is melty and you have lovely grill marks. Slice into wedges and enjoy with a salad!

Ms Boo Dreadful E.V.S.

***

FROM MOROCCO, AN 'OTTOMAN STEAMPUNK TAGINE'

particularly enjoyed in a tiffin box while flying with the Windermere Airship Company the sun glinting on the massed steam launches below

INGREDIENTS
45 ml olive oil, divided
905 g lamb meat, cut into 1 1/2 inch cubes
5 g paprika
0.6 g ground turmeric
1 g ground cumin
0.4 g cayenne pepper
2 g ground cinnamon
0.5 g ground cloves
1 g ground cardamom
5 g kosher salt
0.9 g ground ginger
1 g saffron
2 g garlic powder
2 g ground coriander
220 g onions, cut into 1-inch cubes
5 carrots, peeled, cut into fourths, then sliced lengthwise into thin strips
3 cloves garlic, minced
6 g freshly grated ginger
1 lemon, zested
1 (14.5 ounce) can homemade chicken broth or low-sodium canned broth
20 g sun-dried tomato paste
15 ml honey
8 g cornstarch (optional)
15 ml water (optional)

DIRECTIONS
Place diced lamb in a bowl, toss with 2 tablespoons of the olive oil, and set aside. In a large resealable bag, toss together the paprika, turmeric, cumin, cayenne, cinnamon, cloves, cardamom, salt, ginger, saffron, garlic powder, and coriander; mix well. Add the lamb to the bag, and toss around to coat well. Refrigerate at least 8 hours, preferably overnight.
Heat 1 tablespoon of olive oil in a large, heavy bottomed pot over medium-high heat. Add 1/3 of the lamb, and brown well. Remove to a plate, and repeat with remaining lamb. Add onions and carrots to the pot and cook for 5 minutes. Stir in

the fresh garlic and ginger; continue cooking for an additional 5 minutes. Return the lamb to the pot and stir in the lemon zest, chicken broth, tomato paste, and honey. Bring to a boil, then reduce heat to low, cover, and simmer for 1 1/2 to 2 hours, stirring occasionally, until the meat is tender.
If the consistency of the tagine is too thin, you may thicken it with a mixture of cornstarch and water during the last 5 min

bob basil jet

***

WILD, WILD WESTERN PORK CHOPS

2-6 Pork Chops, Bone In or Out
1 clove Fresh Garlic per Chop, minced as finely as possible
Chili Powder
Fresh Ground Black Pepper
Kosher or Sea Salt
Molasses
Spicy Barbecue Sauce

Set oven on Broil. Allow to heat for 5 minutes. Mix chili powder, black pepper and salt together to taste. Mix molasses and barbecue sauce together to taste. Trim fat off Chops. Vigorously rub 1/2 clove garlic into each side of Chop, season with dry mixture. Rub in further to ensure mixture sticks to meat. Wrap cookie sheet in Aluminum Foil and place chops in single layer on sheet. Place under broiler for 4 minutes. Flip, Broil for additional 4 minutes. Flip again, brush tops liberally with liquid mixture, broil 1-2 minutes. Flip one last time, brush again liberally with liquid mixture, broil 1-2 minutes. Remove from broiler.
Top with Mango or Peach Salsa and serve immediately with garlic cheese mashed potatoes and a cold beer.
Serves as many people as you made Pork Chops (or half that number hungry Engineers!)

(null).exe

***

***

CURRIED CHICKEN WITH FRUIT & PENNE

- 2 Chicken breast halves (skinless, boneless) cut into cubes
- ½ cup each – chopped red peppers - chopped red onions
- ½ granny smith apple, chopped
- ½ cup drained pineapple chunks
- chopped fresh cilantro
- 1 cup heavy cream
- 1 tsp. ground cumin
- ½ tsp. ground coriander
- ½ tsp salt
- 2 tsp curry powder
- ½ tsp each – fresh garlic and ginger, grated
- 2 ½ tbls. Peanut butter
- 2 handfuls peanuts, toasted

Saute onion and red pepper. Add chicken and continue to sauté until lightly browned.
Add spices, then add fruit and cream. Stir in peanut butter and apple, Simmer until apple
is tender, then stir in cilantro and peanuts. Cook pasta while mixture is simmering .Combine mixture with cooked pasta.
This can also be served as a regular curry over rice, preferably basmati.

Note: The spicing can be adjusted to suit individual tastes, but this is a good starting point..

HAC

***

***

MR. GONE'S SANDWICH OF GOOD

by Evelyn Kriete of Jaborwhalky.com

Ingredients:
1 Wheat Bagel (halved)
1 tablespoon Minced Garlic
2-4 tablespoons of Whipped Cream Cheese
1-2 tablespoons Caviar (any kind)
½ tin Sardines
Sliced Black Olives (drained)
Romaine Lettuce
Extra Virgin Olive Oil

Brush bagel lightly with olive oil. Spread garlic on both halves of bagel. Toast bagel in oven or toaster oven. Spread cream cheese on both halves of bagel. Spread caviar on both halves of bagel. Place lettuce on both halves of bagel. Spread a second layer of cream cheese over both pieces of lettuce. Add black olives to one half of bagel; add sardines to other half. Place halves of bagel together and eat; do not cut bagel or else it will fall apart.

Author's Note: I have in fact eaten this sandwich before, and it is delicious.

***

***

G. D. FALKSEN'S SALMAGUNDI SLOP

(serves 4-5 people)

Ingredients:

1 lb. Ground Bison Meat (ground beef can be substituted if bison is not available)

1 lb. Feta Cheese (drained)

1 lb. Spinach

½ cup Minced Garlic

1 pinch Fennel Seeds

1-2 tablespoons Extra Virgin Olive Oil

1 loaf Crusty Bread (optional)

Steps:

   Coat interior of pot with olive oil. Add garlic and fennel. Place pot over a medium heat. Let contents cook for approximately a minute, stirring to prevent garlic from burning. Stir in meat gradually; add meat loosely rather than in large chunks. Allow meat to cook for approximately four to five minutes. Add spinach. Stir contents. Add 1 tablespoon olive oil. Stir contents for three minutes to ensure that contents do not stick. Place top on pot and allow contents to simmer on low heat for five minutes, stirring intermittently. Add drained feta cheese. Stir to prevent cheese from sticking. Continue stirring until cheese has been properly melted, meat has been fully cooked, and contents have been completely mixed. Turn off heat, replace top and let sit for five minutes. Serve in bowls with crusty bread.

***

***

STRAWBERRY LUNCH BURRITOS

(serves 2)

You will need:

Strawberries
2 flour tortillas
4 egg whites
non-stick cooking spray
salt
small skillet

cut up 4 strawberries (2/ tortilla)into small pieces
put aside and spray skillet with non-stick spray
cook egg whites in skillet adding a pinch of salt if desired
flip whites, add (2) strawberries, fold whites over berries and remove from skillet.
place in tortilla and wrap. Repeat and serve.

Kolourz Voss

***

CHAPTER THREE:

Daniel of the HMS Ophelia

SIDE DISHES

***

MAD MACARONI AND CHEESE

* 3 Tbs butter
* 3 Tbs all-purpose flour
* 1/2 tsp salt
* 1 1/2 cup milk
* At least 1 cup grated cheese (I use cheddar and/or pepper-jack for the main cheese and then toss in whatever else I have to hand that I think might work well)
* 1/2 tsp ground mustard seed
* At least 1/4 tsp ground paprika
* Well over a dash of ground cayenne
* Sufficient cooked pasta (more than 1 1/2 cups dry pasta, or enough spaghetti to feed several hungry people

In a saucepan or double-boiler melt the butter, then add salt, mustard, paprika, cayenne, and whatever other spices suit your fancy (I usually put in a good amount of ground black pepper at this point, and pretty much anything without salt will be good, if anything else has salt, decrease the amount of salt added accordingly). Add flour and stir until it is mixed in completely. Slowly add milk, stirring constantly. It is important at this point that if you are not using a double-boiler you stir constantly so as to prevent burning of the sauce. Once all milk has been added and stirred in thoroughly, add grated cheese, and stir until melted in. Turn off heat and cover sauce until pasta is ready.

Prepare pasta to preferred tenderness, drain, and put back in pot/serving vessel. Pour cheese-sauce over pasta and mix until all pasta has a coating of delicious cheesy goodness.

WARNING! If you're a spice-wimp, stick with the mild cheeses, skip the cayenne, and only use 1/8 tsp of paprika. However if you're like me you'll probably spend months experimenting to get the spices just right, and then your friends will say it still wants a little bit more spice (except for that one friend who will forever be afraid of your cooking because the spice is killer...)

I don't know where this recipe originally came from, but I got it from my friend's mother, and then spent the better part of a year trying everything with this recipe; different cheeses (try mozzarella if you want a really smooth, mild sauce), different pastas (radiator pasta holds cheese better than anything else I've found), different spices, etc to the point that as long as I have the basic ingredients I can make this from almost anything that I have at hand. This recipe scales up or down really well; halving everything will make a good hearty meal for one hungry college student, while a doubling or tripling will feed a good potluck crowd. The only tricky thing about scaling up is the amount of pasta needed; you need a lot more pasta for a double-recipe than you do for a single, probably about 2 1/2 times as much, otherwise what you have will be literally swimming in cheese sauce...not that there's anything wrong with that...

theMadTinker

***

RUTABAGA AND POTATO

Ingredients
2 cups water
1 cup milk
3 bullion cubes
3 pounds russet potatoes, peeled, cut into 1 1/2-inch pieces
1/2 rutabaga, peeled, cut into 1/2-inch pieces
3 garlic cloves
1 bay leaf
1 teaspoon dried thyme
½ stick butter, room temperature
1/3 large onion, thinly sliced
Preparation
Butter 13 x 9x2-inch glass baking dish. Combine first 8 ingredients in large pot; bring to boil. Reduce heat, cover partially and simmer until vegetables are very tender, about 30 minutes. Drain well. Transfer vegetables to large bowl. Add ½ stick butter. Using electric mixer, beat mixture until mashed but still chunky. Season with salt and pepper. Transfer mashed vegetables to prepared dish. Grease heavy large skillet over medium-high heat. Add sliced onions and sauté until beginning to brown, about 5 minutes. Reduce heat to medium-low and sauté until onions are tender and golden brown, about 15 minutes. Season with salt and pepper. Spread onions evenly over mashed vegetables. (Casserole can be prepared up to 1 day ahead. Cover and refrigerate.)
Preheat oven to 375° F. Bake casserole uncovered until heated through and top begins to crisp, about 25 minutes.
Steven S.

***

~CREAMY VEGGIES CASSEROLE~

16oz........frozen broccoli, carrot, cauliflower mix
10.5oz.....cream of mushroom soup, undiluted
8oz.........spreadable Garden Veg. cream cheese

Cook veggies according to package. Drain and place in large bowl
In a sauce pan, place soup and cream cheese. Heat enough to mix easily.
Mix well with veggies and place in baking dish. Bake uncovered at 375 degrees
F. for 25 minutes or until bubbly.
I made this just yesterday and, in fact, I am eating the leftovers as we speak. I'm
overjoyed to have the chance to share this with somebody.

K Smithington

***

PUMPKIN PENNE

Makes 6 servings

* Salt
* 1 lb whole wheat penne
* 2 tbsp extra-virgin olive oil
* 3 shallots, finely chopped
* 3 cloves garlic, finely minced
* 2 cups chicken broth
* 1 can (15 oz) pure pumpkin puree
* 1/2 cup fat free half and half
* 1 tsp hot pepper sauce
* 2 pinches ground cinnamon
* 1 pinch nutmeg
* Pepper
* 7 leaves fresh sage, thinly sliced
* Grated Parmesan cheese

Bring a large pot of water to a boil, salt it, add the pasta and cook until al dente.
Drain.

While the pasta is working, in a medium skillet, heat the olive oil over medium heat. Add the shallots and garlic and cook until softened, about 5 minutes. Stir in the chicken broth, pumpkin and cream. Add the hot sauce, cinnamon and nutmeg; season with salt and pepper. Lower the heat and simmer until thickened, about 5 minutes. Stir in the sauce.
Toss the pasta with the sauce and pass the parmesan around the table.

Ms Boo Dreadful E.V.S.

***

ISLAND RICE:

Feeds 10 steampunks

1/2 pound.....white rice
1/3 stick.......butter
1/2 ....red onion
 1 ....red pepper
 1 sprig.......oregano
 3 ....green onions
1/4 bunch.....cilantro
 1 can........Mandarin oranges
 5 oz..........regular raisins
 5 oz..........golden raisins
1/4 tsp.........Sambal (hot garlic chili sauce)
 3 oz..........walnuts
Salt and pepper to taste

Dice onion and pepper. Chop green onions, cilantro, and oregano leaves.
Saute onions in some butter (or saute spray) until opaque, add red pepper and herbs.
Cook rice, add butter and vegetable mix, stir well until butter melts. Add raisins, walnuts, sambal and salt and pepper to taste.
Sorry about the one fourth of a bunch thing, that's what my brother told me to put in. And, to those who don't cook much or know what sambal is, IT IS FREAKIN' HOT!! Thank you.

K Smithington

***

YORKSHIRE PUDDINGS

3/4 cup all-purpose flour
1/2 teaspoon salt
3 eggs
3/4 cup milk
1/2 cup pan drippings from roast prime rib of beef
Preheat the oven to 450 degrees F.
Sift together the flour and salt in a bowl. In another bowl, beat together the eggs and milk until light and foamy. Stir in the dry ingredients just until incorporated. Pour the drippings into a 9-inch pie pan, cast iron skillet, or square baking dish. Put the pan in oven and get the drippings smoking hot. Carefully take the pan out of the oven and pour in the batter.
Put the pan back in oven and cook until puffed and dry, 15 to 20 minutes

Kato

***

EPIPHANY'S DOUBLE BAKED 'TATTERS

* 4 large potatoes
* 8 slices bacon
* 1/2 cup butter milk
* 6 tablespoons butter
* 1/2 teaspoon salt
* 1/4 teaspoon pepper
* 1 cup shredded *SHARP* Cheddar cheese
* 4 chives, diced

Bake potato. The, treat it like you would a jack-o-lantern. Cut off the top, scoop out it's innards. Place tatter innards in a bowl with melted butter, and butter milk, and mash and blend the shit out of it. Mix in salt, pepper, cheese. Put back in potatoes, and top with chives. Place back in oven till warm and cheese is melted. Have a potato top fight with husband while warming. Serve, eat.

47

CHAPTER FOUR:

Crew of the Amaranth:
Matt, Danny, Sasha, Adam, Erin, Laura, Joe, and Jeff

BREADS & ROLLS

***

DINNER ROLLS TO EXPRESS PRIDE IN REFRIGERATOR OWNERSHIP

Part 1
2 1/2 teaspoons dry active yeast, or one packet thereof, dissolved in a little warm milk
1 quart milk (reconstituted powdered milk will do)
1 cup sugar
1 cup mashed potatoes
2/3 cup butter
2 1/2 cups flour

Mix that and let the yeast think about life for two hours or so.

Part 2
2 teaspoons baking powder
1 teaspoon baking soda
2 teaspoons salt
1-2 cups flour

Stir Part 2 into Part 1. Keep this in a big covered bowl in the refrigerator. It will store that way for one month and get sour but still be safe as it goes. Make out rolls as you want them by spooning up globs of it and mixing/kneading more flour into it until it's more like bread-dough and less like batter. You can make the rolls different each time by kneading in whole-wheat flour, crushed nuts, seeds, whole grains, cheese or whatever. Set the rolls to rise for about half an hour or until they double in size. Bake them at 425F for fifteen minutes, or at lower temperatures in with the roast, for longer.

Ben Franklin's Electric Kite

***

***

PUMPERNICKEL
(oh yes, I do revel in the role of the stereotypical German Grin)

Ingredients:

3 packages active dry yeast
1 ½ cups warm water (105 to 115°)
½ cup molasses
4 teaspoons salt
2 tablespoons shortening
2 tablespoons caraway seed
2 ¾ cups rye flour
2 ¾ to 3 ¼ cups flour
Cornmeal

Directions:

Dissolve yeast in warm water. Stir in molasses, salt, shortening, caraway seed, and rye flour. Beat until smooth. Mix in enough white flour to make dough easy to handle. Turn dough onto lightly floured board. Cover; let rest 10 to 15 minutes. Knead until smooth, about 5 minutes. Place in greased bowl; turn greased side up. Cover; let rise in warm place until double, about 1 hour. Punch dough down; round up, cover and let rise again until double, about 40 minutes. Grease baking sheet; sprinkle with cornmeal. Punch dough down; divide in half. Shape each half into round, slightly flat loaf. Place loaves in opposite corners of baking sheet. Cover, let rise 1 hour.

Heat oven to 375°. Bake for 30 to 35 minutes.

Albrecht

***

***

HUDSON BAY BREAD

mix together
1.5 lbs butter
4 cups sugar
2/3 cups corn syrup
2/3 cups honey
couple tsp. real maple syrup for flavor
then mix in
1.5 cups ground nuts (i just chop them super fine)
19 cups oatmeal
 Press mixture in a baking sheet and bake at 350 F for 18 minutes. Press and cut into squares immediately after removing from oven.

Steven S.

***

SPICED CHAI BARMBRACK

FIRST STAGE

Mix together:
1 cup golden raisins or dates
1 cup of raisins
3/4 cup brown sugar
1 cup cold chai tea

Cover these ingredients and leave to soak overnight.

STAGE TWO

Prepare these ingredients:
1 1/2 cups of flour
1 level teaspoon of baking powder
1 egg beaten

1 teaspoon mixed spice

Add the four, baking powder and spice to soaked fruit mixture.Mix in the beaten egg.Spoon into a well greased loaf tin and bake for 1 1/2 hours at 300 degrees Fahrenheit.When cool brush the top with warmed honey for a glazed surface.

Ms Boo Dreadful E.V.S.

***

BREAKFAST BUNS

For decent breakfast buns, you just need a pound of flour, 1 1/2 cups of water, half a cube of yeast, some sugar and some salt.

First of all, you need a starter. Take the yeast, some sugar, some flour(2 teaspoons) and a pinch of water and mix thoroughly. Make sure it's smooth. Let it rise for an hour. In the meantime, you should mix the salt(about 1 tablespoon) into the flour. Add the risen starter to that, add 1 1/2 cups of water, knead until smooth. Cover it and let it rise for another hour. In the end, form out the buns by rolling balls from the dough. Add a pinch of water to the balls' surface, roll them in flour and cut the surface. One cut, should be pretty deep. Put them on a floured tray and into a pre-heated oven. Most ovens should be set to 425 degrees F (220 degrees C). Let them bake for twenty minutes. Enjoy them warm or cold, but not completely hot.

ElShoggotho

***

***

BANANA BREAD

1 cup sugar
1/2 cup butter
3 ripe bananas
2 well beaten eggs
8 tablespoons milk
2 cups flour
1 teaspoon baking soda
1/2 teaspoon salt (optional)
1 cup walnuts (optional)

Cream butter and sugar. Add eggs and bananas Mix thoroughly. Add milk, flour and baking soda. Bake at 350°F for 1 hour.

Jo

***

KLAUDE DAVENPORT'S BASIC SCONE RECIPE

2 cups self-rising flour
1/2 teaspoon baking soda
3/4 cup buttermilk
berries, fruit or nuts to add as desired

Heat oven to 350 degrees. Sift self-rising flour into mixing bowl, form into a tiny flour volcano. In separate bowl stir baking soda into buttermilk until it begins to foam. Pour this mixture into the center well of your flour volcano (roaring/exploding noises should be made at this time). If you wish, additional ingredients of berries, fruit or nuts can be added at this time. Klaude's recommends sacrificing 1/2 cup of blueberries to the mouth of your flour volcano. Stir with a fork until just enough flour has been incorporated to create a very soft dough. Gather into a ball and place on a lightly floured surface. Working as quickly as possible, with minimal agitation to dough, form into circle shape. Cut or prick wedge outline for easier separation post-baking. Bake for 10 to 12 minutes in upper third of oven. Wrap in napkin and serve with clotted cream, honey and your favorite tea.

Makes 8-10 scones.
Klaude Davenport

***

EMMETT DAVENPORT'S CREAM TEA CAKES OR "UP HIGH BISCUITS"

INGREDIENTS:
1 cup butter or margarine
3/4 cup white sugar
1 1/4 cups all-purpose flour
2/3 (3 ounce) package instant vanilla pudding
1 egg
1 pinch salt

DIRECTIONS:
Preheat oven to 350 degrees F (175 degrees C).
In a medium-sized mixing bowl, beat margarine and sugar until very soft. Add beaten egg, instant vanilla pudding mix, flour, and salt. Knead well on a floured surface.
Roll out and cut with a plain biscuit cutter. Bake for 10 minutes or until pale brown.

***

ENGLISH TEA CAKES

1 cup sugar
1 cup butter
4 eggs, unbeaten
1 cup flour
1 cup currants

Beat sugar and butter together until creamy. Add eggs, one at a time, mix well. Blend in the flour and currants. Pour batter into a baking pan/cookie sheet lined with well-greased paper. Bake at 350 F. for thirty minutes. Cut into small squares while warm.

So simple and they go great with tea for the victorians, or rum for the Ophelia crew.

K Smithington

***

***

BROWN SCONES

2 cups self-raising flour
3 tbsp olive oil margarine
1/2 cup 2% milk
pinch of salt

Sieve the flour into a bowl and rub in the butter quickly and lightly with the fingertips. Add the salt and then, using a round-bladed knife, mix in the milk a little at a time. With floured hands knead lightly to a soft dough, adding a little more milk if necessary. Roll out evenly but lightly about one finger thick on a floured board. Cut out with a pastry cutter using a quick sharp motion, but do not twist or the scones will distort as they bake. Cook on a greased baking sheet near the top of a pre-heated oven at 425&degree;F for 12-15 mins.

These scones are best baked fresh for tea as they go stale very quickly. Brown scones are made in exactly the same way, substituting wholemeal flour for half the white flour. For fruit scones add a tablespoonful of superfine sugar and two tablespoonfuls of dried fruit before adding the milk.

Ms Boo Dreadful E.V.S.

CHAPTER FIVE:

Nathaniel of the HMS Ophelia

SOUPS & SALADS

***

SLOW CHILI

1 Shoulder Arm Roast (pork) or Chuck Roast (beef) - (something tough)
5-6 med. yellow onions
1 med. can crushed plum tomatoes
(all approximate - adjust to taste - I measure by eye:)
1 tbsp chopped garlic.
2 tbsp chili powder
1 tbsp cround cumin
1 tsp fround coriander
1 tsp dried oregano (though fresh would be good too...)
1 tsp hot Hugarian paprika
pinch red pepper flakes
pinch (literally) garam masala or curry powder
2 tsp Sriracha Thai chili sauce OR cayenne hotsauce (Crystal or Texas Pete)
salt
black pepper

olive oil
~ 2 cups Chicken stock
1-2 cans black beans (drain and rinse)

usually use a dutch-oven type soup pot, but electric crock pot works surprisingly
well

remove excess fat and cut meat into approx 2.5" cubes.
thin-slice onions
sear meat in olive oil over med-hig heat - brown the hell out of it. Add to pot.
lower heat to med, saute 3 medium onions until very heavily
  caramelized - darker, the better. when dark brown, add garlic, saute a minute
or so. add to pot.
 heat more oil in saute pan, add dried spices - chili powder, cumin, coriander,
paprika,
  pepper flakes, pinch of garam masala (be careful here - it shouldnt taste like
curry just a touch
 of "hmmm.. what's that flavor??") -
brown in oil about 1-2 minutes, until they form a thick paste and darken.
 Occasionally, a gas mask comes in handy for this step.
 deglaze / rinse pan withh chicken stock and add to pot. add enough stock to just
barely cover the

meat. Cover.
 bring to boil, lower to simmer for approx. 2 hrs.
  (at one point, the meat will resemble hard, nasty little golfballs - it's not ruined -
  that's supposed to happen. Meat will get tender, sauce will thicken.)
When meat softens after "golfball" stage, add reserved onions, hot sauce and
crushed tomatoes.
   Allow to cook until meat falls apart - approx. another 2-3 hrs.
 Remove meat, skim any floating fat, shred/chop finely and return to skimmed
liquid
 add black beans (rinse of the salty, slimy packing liquid first) and heat through,
  allow sauce to reduce and thicken.

Started out as a Cuban Ropa Vieja recipe and evolved into chili. A TINY bit of
curry powder makes
an amazing difference. What you had MAY have had fresh basil, too. I don't
remember.

Cap'n Harlock

***

BEEF STEW RECIPE

3-5 lb chuck roast, fat reserved
1 c. chopped onion
1 bottle dark beer
1 packet onion soup mix
water
4 medium potatoes
6 medium carrots
two medium onions

Take a 3-5 pound chuck roast. Remove fat. Cut meat into approximately 1"
cubes. While cutting meat up, fry removed fat in large saucepan that can be
tightly sealed. Add a cup of chopped onions and brown them almost burning
them with the fat. Add cubed beef and brown. Remove fat and throw away.
Deglaze pan with one beer, preferably a dark beer. Add onion soup mix with
enough water to cover beef and cover pan, cook on low heat until beef is tender,
about an hour.

While cooking beef, peel 4 medium potatoes, 6 medium carrots and two medium onions. Chop into approximately 1" chunks. Place in stewpot with enough water to cover by an inch. Add herbs and spices to taste, we usually use tarragon, sage, thyme and garlic. Cook until just tender.

Add beef to cooked vegetables. Cook together for 1/2 hour.

For a good addition, take unpeeled garlic bulbs and cook with vegetables. Take cooked garlic, squeeze out soft cloves and mix with softened butter. Great on homemade bread.

Hexidecima

***

CHILI

3 pounds ground beef (preferably the fattiest you can get)

1 medium can chopped tomatoes and green chiles

1 medium can refried black beans

2 large cans of tomato sauce

1 meduim can of pink beans

2 cups of chopped onions

2 tablespoons of ground cumin

2 tablespoons of chili powder

3 cloves of minced garlic

Fry burger and onions in large pot. Drain off extra fat. Add everything else. Cook until heated through. Tastes like it's been cooked for days.

hexidecima

***

SEAFOOD CHOWDER

1 small can crabmeat (not surimi/krab!) (reserve liquid)

2 pounds white-fleshed fish, like cod, flounder, perch, catfish, etc.

1/2 pound sea scallops

2 small cans chopped clams (reserve liquid)

1 small can minced clams (reserve liquid)

1 large can baby clams (reserve liquid)

4 medium potatoes, peeled and cubed

4 medium onions, peeled and diced

2" cube of salt pork (not bacon!)

1/2 pound (2 sticks) butter (yes, 2 sticks. Do not use anything else!)

3/4 cup flour

4 cups whole milk

1 cup heavy cream

Dice salt pork. In a large skillet, cook it slowly to render out the fat. Add onions and cook until translucent. Add seafood and 1 stick of butter. Heat, make sure butter is melted. Sift flour over seafood/butter/salt pork mixture, mix in well. Let cook a couple of minutes. Add reserved liquid from seafood. Heat to thicken.

In large pot (think stewpot, usually biggest in a set of pots), put milk, cream and potatoes and remaining stick of butter. Cook potatoes until able to be pierced by a fork.

Add seafood mixture. Heat through. Wonderful immediately and even better after a day or two.

hexidecima

***

MOM'S LIME AND CHEESE SALAD

1 lg. package lime gelatin
1 20 oz can crushed pineapple - drained
1 8oz pkg cream cheese - softened
1 c. chopped walnuts
1 c. chopped celery
1 container Cool Whip

Prepare gelatin according to package directions. Chill. Cream together pineapple and cream cheese. Add to thickened but not set gelatin. Stir in celery and nuts. Spread Cool Whip on top.

Lily

***

MARDI GRAS DINNER SALAD
(serves two)

You will need

Spinach leaves
Carrots (sliced or shredded)
Broccoli crowns (fresh)
1 Eggplant
2 vine ripened tomatoes
1 bell pepper
1 zuccini
1 yellow squash
1 can California Ripe olives (black)
1 cup of chopped pecans
1/2-1 cup sliced pepperoncini peppers
1 can albacore tuna in water
non-stick cooking spray
Miracle Whip or salad dressing equivalent
pickle relish
shredded swiss cheese
*Onion or onion powder optional

Med. skillet
spatula
bowl

Cut eggplant into 6 long slices, zuccini and squash into 10 long slices each. Chop 1.5 tsp. bell pepper. spray medium skillet with non-stick cooking spray and set burner to medium-high heat. Mix eggplant, zuccini,squash, and pepper in and stir evenly. Add 1 can of California Ripe black olives (drained)and slow brown veggies, stirring occasionally.

In the bowl, mix one drained can of albacore tuna with 1 tablespoon of Miracle Whip, 1/4 tsp. pickle relish, dash of onion powder. Thoroughly mix. Add 1/2 of this to the skillet and cook until lightly browned.
Remove form heat.

On 2 plates, arrange spinach leaves in a circular pattern. Using the broccoli crowns and carrots, make a halo within the spinach. Place zuccini in 5 long pieces per plate in a ring coming from the center. Repeat with yellow squash. Finally, place three pieces of eggplant stemming from the center of the plate. Follow with a dollop of browned tuna salad in the center of each plate. Add diced tomatoes to the top of each salad for colour, then drizzle pecans over top to complete.
Use desired salad dressing

Kolourz Voss

CHAPTER SIX:

Dread Cap'n Robert of the HMS Ophelia

DESERTS, COOKIES, & CANDIES

***
CHERRY-CHEESE PIE:

1 8 oz. package cream cheese
1/2 cup sugar
2 eggs
1/3 cup chopped nuts
1 teaspoon vanilla extract

Blend all of the above. Pour into partially baked pie crust. Bake at 350 degrees for ten minutes.

2 cans cherry pie filling
whipped cream

Spread cherry filling over cooled pie. Top with whipped cream. Chill.

Rose Streiffe

***

MISS CORA EWAN'S OATMEAL COOKIES
invented in Cuba, Illinois, around 1918 (probably)

Cream together:
1 1/2 cup sugar
1 cup lard

Oh, very well, you may use butter. In fact they are better that way, but I beg you to take a stand against vegetable shortening, margarine, and perculiar emulsifications with complete sentances such as "This Better Not Be Butter!" pressed into service as their names.

Dry part:
3 cups flour
3 cups oatmeal
2 teaspoons cinnamon
1 teaspoon clove
1/2 teaspoon nutmeg
2 teaspoons baking soda
1 pound (about 2 cups) raisins

Third part:
2 eggs beaten together in a cup, then add
Milk until you've got a cup of liquid.

Mix the three parts together, possibly with the aid of a powerful machine.

The venerable recipe card says to roll the dough into balls the size of hickory nuts. I am not entirely sure how large a hickory nut is, and roll them the size of walnuts. I bake them at 375F for around ten minutes, on greased sheets.

Ben Franklin's Electric Kite

***

PIE CRUST THAT MY MOTHER LEARNED ON NEWFOUNDLAND

3 cups flour
1 cup lard

Again, very well, use butter. It will be crispier and lighter if you use lard and deliciously buttery-tasting if you use butter. Once again, please, no vegetable shortening, much less "You Expect Me To Believe This Is Butter?!"

Mix flour and butter together with a fork or one of those wire pastry-tools, until you've got a bowlful of what looks like fine sand.

add:
1 egg, beaten in a cup with
1 tablespoon of white vinegar. Add
Water until you have 3/4 cups of liquid.

Mix it until it is mixed, and stop. Divide it into three more or less equal sized balls. Roll it out on a floured surface. Expect it to take on some flour as you go.

It is helpful to imagine its microscopic workings as you mix and roll. The dough is made up of tiny balls of flour and butter suspended densely in liquid. When you roll it out, the balls smear into little discs suspended overlapping-scale-wise in the liquid. In the oven, the liquid becomes lovely steam and pushes these scales apart, creating the flakey texture. If you over-roll the dough, you'll push the flour-and-butter balls into one solid sheet and the liquid will end up on the surface. The results on baking will be hard, tasteless and brittle. Go lightly.

This recipe makes three crusts for ordinary-sized pies, so you can make one pie with a top-crust and one without, or three without. This is awkward, but the ball of unused dough will keep well in a freezer. You can instead make a couple of fold-over pies with it, filled with any extra pie-filling, or leftover stew, or a few spoons of pizza-sauce and pepperoni and cheese.

Bake it the way your pie-recipe suggests, it is well-behaved. It tastes well with any filling, be it cherries, custard, egg or steak. It's also quite nice to wrap a small roast, seared and sprinkled with herbs, in it and proceed as normal.

Ben Franklin's Electric Kite

***

PRESS IN PIE CRUST

2 c. flour, heaped
Pinch of salt
1/2 c. oil
1/2 cup milk,combined with oil

Stir quickly; roll between wax paper. Bake at 450 degrees for 10 minutes to use prebaked crust; or, bake per specific pie directions. Makes 2 crusts.

This crust is so-o-o easy! It makes cinnamon rolls a joy to bake. Just mix above ingredients and roll dough between wax paper in circle. Cover top of crust with butter; sprinkle sugar, cinnamon and finely chopped nuts on top of butter. Cut into pie shape and roll, beginning at point, and rolling to the outer edge. Bake at 450 degrees for about 10 minutes and ENJOY!

Ms Boo dreadful E.V.S.

***

BREAD PUDDING WITH BERRY SAUCE

Custard
1 quart whole milk
1/2 pound granulated sugar
1 vanilla bean, split
4 large eggs
8 large egg yolks

Pudding
2 ounces golden raisins
2 fluid ounces rum
6 to 7 ounces stale brioche bread, cut into 1/2-inch cubes
3 ounces unsalted butter, melted
1 and 1/4 quarts custard (see above)

For custard: Bring milk to a boil with sugar and vanilla bean. Beat eggs and yolks together. Slowly add milk mixture to eggs, whisking briskly, until liquid (add milk to eggs, a little at a time or the heat will scramble the eggs). Once combined, strain into a clean bowl (just in case you did manage to scramble the eggs). Remove vanilla bean and rinse. Reserve for another use.

For pudding: Bring raisins to a boil in a large pan of water and drain. Place them in a small container and pour in 1 ounce of the rum; allow to soak for at least an hour. (The raisins will keep indefinately and can be made well ahead of time.)

Scatter the raisins in the bottom of a gratin dish. Toss bread with melted butter and place in the dish on top of the raisins.

Whisk the remaining ounce of rum in to the custard and pour over bread, making sure to moisten everything. Allow bread to soak up custard for roughly 1/2 hour to an hour.

Bake custard at 300F in a pan of water filled approximately halfway up the side of the gratin dish for 45 minutes to an hour, or until the custard has set and the bread is beginning to brown slightly.

Berry Sauce for Bread Pudding
1 pint strawberries

1 pint blackberries or raspberries
sugar to taste
sweet wine to taste (optional)

Cut and stem strawberries. Lightly rinse in cold water, drain, and place in small bowl. Add blackberries and/or raspberries to strawberries. Add enough sugar to sweeten the berries and to begin drawing out the natural juices. Add sweet wine to taste.

Allow berries to mascerate in refrigerator until there is mostly juice and very little berry left. Puree remaining solids with a hand blender. Serve over bread pudding.

Cybele13

***

CARADAMOM SHORTBREAD

3/4 cup sugar

1 1/2 cups butter (don't use anything else!)

4 cups flour

1 tsp ground cardamom

Cream butter and sugar together with cardamom. Add flour one cup at a time and mix well. Press into 9"x13" pan. Bake at 325 degrees (farhenheit) for 35-40 minutes. Doubling this recipe will fill 4 8"x8" pans, useful for bake sales or snacks for demos.

Hexidecima

***

CHOCOLATE TOFFEE CHIP COOKIES RECIPE

2 1/4 cups all-purpose flour

1 tsp baking soda

1 tsp salt

1 cup (2 sticks, 1/2 pound) butter, softened

3/4 cup sugar

3/4 cup brown sugar

1 tsp vanilla extract

2 eggs

1 cup semi-sweet chocolate chips

1 cup toffee chips

The order mixed does make a difference in the texture of the cookies.

Combine flour, baking soda, salt, in small bowl.

Beat softened butter, eggs and vanilla in large mixer bowl. Add sugar, brown sugar, beating continously.

Gradually beat in flour mixture. Stir in chips.

Drop by rounded tablespoonfuls on to ungreased cookie sheets.

Bake in preheated 375 degree (Farhenheit) oven for 9-11 minutes or until golden brown. Let stand for 2 minutes; remove to wire racks to cool completely. Store in sealed container. Add a piece of bread to keep cookies moist.

hexidecima

***

GOBS RECIPE

These are real gobs, not the cake/icing fakes, usually called "whoopie pies", that most people think are gobs.

Cookie part:

2 cups sugar

1/2 cup vegatable shortening (like Crisco, etc)

2 eggs

1 cup soured milk (1 tbsp vinegar to 1 cup whole milk)

1 cup boiling water

1 tsp vanilla

4 cups flour

2 tsp baking soda

1/2 tsp baking powder

1/4 tsp salt

Cream together sugar, shortening, and eggs in large bowl. Sift dry ingredients in separate bowl. Add soured milk, boiling water, vanilla and dry ingredients. Refrigerate batter for at least an hour. Drop by rounded teaspoonfuls onto ungreased cookie sheets. Bake in preheated 450 degree (Farenheit) oven for 5-7 minutes. Test for doneness with toothpick.
Filling:

In a medium saucepan, stir 1 cup cold milk into 5 tbsp flour. Cook on low heat until thick. Cool. Cream 1 cup vegatable shortening with 1 cup of sugar and 1 tsp vanilla. Add to flour mixture and beat until fluffy.

Spread filling between two cookies.

hexidecima

***

GOOP RECIPE

Otherwise known as Chocolate Coconut Balls. This is Daren's mom's recipe. If you make angelfood cake from scratch, it's a great way to use up the egg yolks. It comes out very much like a ganache.

1 cup flour

1 cup sugar

1/4 tsp salt

1 cup whole milk

4 egg yolks

4 tbsp butter (don't use anything else!)

2 tsp vanilla extract

12 oz. semi-sweet chocolate chips

1 cup chopped nuts and/or shredded coconut (optional)

Sift flour, sugar, salt together in small bowl. In double-boiler, put milk, yolks and butter, heat until butter melts. Add flour mixture. Cook until thick (takes about 10 minutes). Remove from heat and stir in chocolate chips and vanilla. Refrigerate for several hours. Roll into balls and roll into nuts/coconut, if desired.

Hexidecima

***

DEVONSHIRE FAUX CREAM

1 cup heavy whipping cream
 1/4 cup softened cream cheese
1 heaping tablespoon sugar
1 teaspoon vanilla extract

The directions are the same for both cream recipes: Combine all ingredients in a medium bowl and beat with a mixer until stiff. Refrigerate until ready to use. Best when prepared and served the same day. Makes 1 1/4 to 1 1/2 cups.

Ms Boo dreadful E.V.S.

***

DANDELION JELLY

1 qt. dandelion flowers
1 qt. water
1 tsp. lemon juice
1 box Sure-Jell

1. Cook together for 3 minutes the flowers and water.
2. Strain and save juice.
3. Follow directions on Sure-Jell box using dandelion water.
4. Bring to a boil, then add 4 1/2 cups sugar and lemon juice.

Ms. Boo Dreadful E.V.S.

FUEL FOR THE BOILER

***

CHOCOLATE HAZELNUT ROASTED APPLES

You will need four apples
a jar of chocolate-hazelnut spread (Nutella)
 and about a cup of your favorite chopped nuts (I use hazelnuts or filberts if I can get them, or pecans or walnuts do just as well.)

Core your apples, being sure to get out all the seeds, place cored apples on a buttered pan (use one with an edge to catch any juice leakage.) take about four tablespoons of the spread, and mix with the nuts, then put 1/4th of the mixture into the holes left when you cored them. Bake at 350 degrees Fahrenheit until the apples are soft (this will vary depending on your type of apples, anywhere from ten minutes to thirty, but generally, if the peel of the apple looks crinkly, they are done.)

These are absolutely delicious, easy to make, and serve four very satisfyingly!

The Hon. Luc Du Rette

***

PECAN PIE

A good pie recipe for a pecan pie, but using walnuts or hazelnuts will make it even richer and more tasty:
You need:
three eggs,
 a cup of sugar (the "raw" kind improves the taste)
a cup of dark corn syrup (the darker, the better)
2 tablespoons of butter
one cap ful of the vanilla extract (try to get the real stuff, it's worth it!)
one and a half cups of your choice of nuts, chopped (it makes a different look than the classic pecan pie with whole nuts, but makes the flavor better)
and one deep dish pie shell (it's OK to cheat and buy cheap, as long as it is not broken.)

Beat your eggs, then add everything but the nuts, and stir until smooth. add our nuts, and stir them in, then pour mixture into crust.
Bake in a 350 degree Fahrenheit oven about an hour, it will be done when the pie springs back when you tap it in the center.

A yummy variation is to add chocolate chips to replace part of the nuts, but no more than 1/4th, or you won't have enough nuts to cover the top.

This started off as the recipe on the back of the Karo syrup bottle, with very little variation.

The Hon. Luc Du Rette

***

PINEAPPLE UPSIDE-DOWN BISCUITS

1 (10-ounce) can crushed pineapple
1/2 cup packed Dark brown sugar
1/4 cup (1/2 stick) butter, at room temperature
10 maraschino cherries
1 (12-ounce) package refrigerated buttermilk biscuits (10 count)or one packet instant corn bread mix.

Preheat the oven to 400 degrees F.

Grease 10 cups of a muffin tin. Strain the can of crushed pineapple, save juice for later. Combine the pineapple, sugar, and butter, and mix well. Divide the pineapple mixture among the muffin cups. Place a cherry in the center of each muffin cup, making sure cherry hits bottom of cup. Place 1 biscuit in each cup on top of sugar and pineapple mixture. Spoon 1 teaspoon reserved pineapple juice over each biscuit. Bake for 12 to 15 minutes, or until golden. Cool for 2 minutes. Invert the pan onto a plate to release the biscuits. Serve warm.
Alternately, you may use cornbread mix instead of the canned biscuits for a more southern feel. Its really fun to use organic blue corn cornmeal!

Ms. Boo dreadful E.V.S.

FUEL FOR THE BOILER

***

WALNUT WAFERS

3   heaping tbsp. flour
1/8 tsp. salt
1   cup brown sugar
2   eggs
1   cup chopped walnuts

Beat eggs very well with mixer (not with whisk, that will take forever!) Gradually beat sugar into eggs. Fold in flour. Drop into small blobs on parchment lined baking sheet and bake at 400 degrees F. for about five minutes. These are very thin crisp wafers.

K Smithington

***

BROWN SUGAR SHORT BREAD SQUARES

2   cups flour
1/2 cup   butter
1/2 cup   light brown sugar
1   egg

Cream the butter and sugar together. Add the egg and mix well. Blend in the flour and knead the dough until smooth. Roll medium thin into square baking pan and cut into squares. Bake at 400 degrees F. until light brown.
I'm sorry I don't have the baking time for those short bread squares. It's been a long time since I made those, i can't remember how long, my recipe doesn't say how long.... guess people will have to keep watch over it.

K Smithington

***

O-MOCHI

Ingredients:

   * Glutinous rice (Sticky, Japanese, Mochi, Sweet, Waxy, Botan or Pearl rice)
   * Sugar
   * Warm water
   * Flour
   * Optional filling/flavoring (red bean paste, strawberry, banana or ice cream –
be creative; if it's sweet and fits inside the mochi, it probably will be delicious!)

Considering the fact that the traditional way of making mochi is fairly labor intensive, it is normally produced in fairly large quantities. Often enough for an extended family, sometimes enough for an entire neighborhood. As a rule of thumb however, the following quantities will be used per pound of rice: 2 ½ cups of sugar, 2 cups of water. The flour and filling can easily be 'eyeballed'.

Tools of the trade:

   * Kine – a large wooden mallet (you might want two or three for larger quantities).
   * Uru – a heavy wooden mortar.
   * An ordinary mortar and pestle would work, but why on Earth would you want to make mochi the hard way if you don't even get to smash anything with a big hammer?
   * A rice steamer.
   * One or more minions – either to do the laborious pounding, or to timely turn the goo before the mallet comes crashing back down.

Directions:

Soak the rice and steam it so it becomes really sticky. Use the time the rice is steaming to soak the mallet in water, this helps the rice from sticking to it. Also rinse the mortar with water. When the rice is steamed, place the mass in the uru or mortar while still hot and add a little water. Then start pounding away. Try to pound in a steady rhythm as someone has to reach under the hammer to occasionally twist the mass of rice! For larger quantities you can have two or even three people pounding away, with another person responsible for turning

77

the rice mass. Be careful not to crush his/her hands! Gradually add the sugar and keep hammering until the rice is completely broken and forms a consistent goo. Add water as desired, but don't let it get soggy. Make sure the mass gets flipped over a number of times. When the mass reaches the consistency of thin clay, it is ready for the next step. Break off fist-sized lumps and kneed them into balls. Cover the outside with flour to keep them from sticking to your hands. If desired, add filling at this stage.

Mochi are best eaten when fresh and warm, although they can be kept for fairly long periods. If the outer shell dries, a little water and some gentle kneading does wonders!

Akumabito

***

APPLE & MACADAMIA NUT CRISP

Makes an 8 x 8 inch pan
Prep time: 1 hour

Ingredients:

1/3 cup all-purpose flour
1/4 cup sugar
1/4 cup firmly packed brown sugar
1/4 cup chopped macadamia nuts
1/2 tsp ground cinnamon
1/2 tsp grated nutmeg
2 tbsp chilled butter, cut into small pieces
5 cups thinly sliced peeled apples
1/4 cup apricot preserves

Method:

Preheat oven to 375° F. Lightly butter an 8 x 8 inch baking dish.

Combine the flour, sugars, macadamia nuts, cinnamon and nutmeg in a bowl; stir well. Cut in butter until mixture resembles coarse meal; set aside.

Toss apple slices with apricot preserves. Spread into the prepared baking dish and sprinkle evenly with the flour mixture. Bake for 35 minutes or until bubbly and golden.

Serve warm with French vanilla frozen yogurt.

HAC

***

EPIPHANY'S RUST RED VELVET CUPCAKES WITH BUTTER CREAM FROSTING

* 4 tablespoon unsweetened cocoa powder
* 2 ounce red food coloring
* 1 cup buttermilk
* 1 teaspoon salt
* 1 teaspoon vanilla extract
* 1 cup oil
* 1 1/2 cup white sugar
* 2 eggs
* 2-1/2 cups all-purpose flour, sifted
* 1 1/2 teaspoon baking soda
* 1 teaspoon white vinegar

Butter Cream Icing

* 2/3 cup butter, softened
* 1 teaspoon vanilla extract
* 4 cups confectioners' sugar
* 2 tablespoon cream
* 1 teaspoon Almond extract

Mix a paste of the cocoa and food coloring. Set it aside. Mix the buttermilk, salt and vanilla. Set it aside. In a large bowl, cream together the shortening and sugar until fluffy. Whip in the eggs one at a time, then stir in the cocoa mixture. Beat in the buttermilk mixture alternately with the flour, mixing just until incorporated. Stir together baking soda and vinegar, then gently fold into the cake batter. Bake at 350 for 10-15 minutes, depending on cup cake pan. While cooking, mix the icing ingredients together and top the cup cakes once they are cooled.

CHAPTER SEVEN:

Crew of the HMS Chronabelle:
Grand Duchess, Captain Mouse, and Lady Almira

THIS, THAT, & THE OTHER

***

KAISERLICHES LUFTSCHIFFKORPS RATION PACK
(one day, one person, light to medium load)

Four slices of pumpernickel or other "real" bread (yea, I mean this heavy, chewy stuff)
Four slices of ham/cheese/saussage/soyproduct (whatever you prefer)
Two Landjäger or similar "snack sausages" (or comparable snacks for vegetarians and vegans)
Two apples (or, if you've just stopped by in Istanbul, take a couple of figs or dates)
one bar of dark chocolate (20 grams)
Optional flask of recreational beverage
Flask of water.

Put two slices of ham/cheese between two slices of bread. Cut in half.
Place your four halfs in lunchbox or similar container.
Place snacks in container.
Wrap chocolate in tinfoil or parchement paper, place in container.
close container.
Put container in knapsack.
Place fruit in knapsack.
Place flask with RB in breastpocket.
Take flask of water and knapsack.
Go on to new adventures.

Albrecht

***

MASTER OATMEAL RECIPE

Makes 6 cups.
The amount of water you need may depend on the brand of oats you buy, or how creamy you like your oatmeal.

• 2 tbsp. unsalted butter

• 2 c. steel-cut oats, uncooked

• 6 to 7 c. boiling water

•1/8 to 1/4 tsp. salt

• Milk, cream or toppings of your choice

Directions

In a large heavy-bottomed pot with a lid, melt the butter over medium-high heat. Add the oats and toast, stirring often, until the oats smell nutty and butterscotchy, about 3 to 4 minutes.

Stir in 6 cups boiling water and salt. Reduce heat to medium and cover. Stir frequently -- every 5 minutes at first, then every minute or so as the oatmeal thickens, reducing the heat gradually to medium-low and adding up to a cup more boiling water if mixture is too thick.

About 15 minutes after you've added the water, taste the oatmeal; it should be al dente, but not hard or raw-tasting. For chewy oatmeal, cook about 20 minutes; for creamy oatmeal, cook for up to 35 minutes. Serve with desired accompaniments.

If making in advance: Let oatmeal cool completely. Store, tightly covered, in the refrigerator for up to 7 days.

To prepare leftovers, use 1 cup cooked oatmeal per serving. Warm over medium-high heat in a saucepan with 1/2 cup water or milk per serving until bubbling and smooth.

Note, the steel-cut oats are a must. It tastes fantastic, and keeps well. I prefer mine with a healthy addition of brown sugar, but try whatever you wish. It is just

the thing to heat up on the boilers during the morning shift tending the firebox on the old airship.
G. S. Cephias

***

CRANBERRY GELATIN RELISH

1 pound pkg of fresh cranberries
1 cup of chopped celery
1 8 oz. tin of crushed pineapple
1 cup of chopped walnuts or pecans, as desired
2 packages of unflavored gelatin (or two packages of a flavored gelatin mix; I like to use black cherry, for color, but any red colored flavor will do just fine)
2 cups of sugar

Take the cranberries, and run them through a meat grinder (the old fashioned kind), saving the juices produced.
(You can use other methods to chop them, but the texture produced will differ.)
(You can also do this with the celery and nuts, to save chopping, if you do so, I recommend saving the celery until last, to help "clear" the grinder, if you do this, again, save the juices.)
Spread the result in a pan, and cover with sugar, and set aside in your icebox while you prepare the gelatin.
To prepare the gelatin, take the juices from the cranberries (and celery, if you ground it), and drain the excess juices from your tin of pineapple into this. (You should have about a cup of juice, but it doesn't much matter.)
Heat the juice to boiling, and bloom your gelatin in it.
Take your pan out of the icebox, add your pineapple, and then mix in your dissolved gelatin.
Pour into glass bowls, and return to icebox until solid, about an hour, but overnight is best.
Makes a beautiful dessert or side dish (It truly does!)

The recipe is an old family one, my additions or comments are in the parentheses.

The Hon. Luc Du Rette

***

CHIMICHURRI RECIPE

An Argentinian sauce for grilled meat. It's wonderful on just about anything. This is just my version, everyone has their personal recipe.

1 large bunch (a good handful) of cilantro

1 large bunch (a good handful) of parsley

8 cloves of garlic

1/4 cup lime juice

1/4 cup vinegar (white, wine, apple cider)

2/3 cup vegetable oil

Salt to taste.

Place cilantro and parsley in food processor with chopping blade. Blitz until finely chopped. Add garlic. Blitz again. Add juice, vinegar, and oil. Blitz again. Add salt to taste.

Hexidecima

***

LAVENDER SUGAR

1/3 cup fresh or dried lavender flowers
1 cup sugar
Layer the lavender and sugar in a small airtight container.
Seal and store in a dark place for about 2 weeks.
Shake well to combine lavender and sugar.
Recipe can be doubled.

Ms Boo Dreadful E.V.S.

***

HOMEMADE ROSEWATER - QUICK & EASY RECIPE

For every 1 firmly packed cup of rose petals, pour 2 cups boiling water over top. Cover and steep until the liquid is cool. Strain, squeeze out the liquid from the petals, and refrigerate the rose water in a sterilized jar.

Ms Boo Dreadful E.V.S.

***

SIMPLE SYRUP FOR BEVERAGES

Bring 2 cups of plain cold tap water to a boil. Stir in 2 cups of plain granulated sugar. Turn the heat to low and stir constantly until the sugar dissolves completely.
To test if the sugar is completely dissolved, use a metal spoon to scoop up a small bit of the syrup. Tilt it over the pan and watch carefully. You shouldn't be able to see any crystals in the liquid.

At this point you can add flavorings; add about a tablespoon of any liquid extract. You can also stir in 1 tablespoon corn syrup to help ensure the syrup stays smooth.

Let the syrup cool to room temperature, then pour into a clean glass jar and store in the refrigerator.

Ms Boo Dreadful E.V.S.

CHAPTER EIGHT:

Human crew of the HMS Labyrinth:
Ms Boo Dreadful Captain, and Wrong Side Spooky, Navigations Officer

CONVERSION CHARTS

& RESOURCES

CONVERSION TABLE FOR COOKING

U.S. TO METRIC
CAPACITY
1/5 teaspoon = 1 ml
1 teaspoon = 5 ml
1 tablespoon = 15 ml
1 fluid oz. = 30 ml
1/5 cup = 50 ml
1 cup = 240 ml
2 cups (1 pint) = 470 ml
4 cups (1 quart) = .95 liter
4 quarts (1 gal.) = 3.8 liters

WEIGHT
1 oz. = 28 grams
1 pound = 454 grams

METRIC TO U.S.
CAPACITY
1 militers = 1/5 teaspoon
5 ml = 1 teaspoon
15 ml = 1 tablespoon
30 ml = 1 fluid oz.
100 ml = 3.4 fluid oz.
240 ml = 1 cup
1 liter = 34 fluid oz.
1 liter = 4.2 cups
1 liter = 2.1 pints
1 liter = 1.06 quarts
1 liter = .26 gallon

WEIGHT

1 gram = .035 ounce
100 grams = 3.5 ounces
500 grams = 1.10 pounds
1 kilogram = 2.205 pounds
1 kilogram = 35 oz.

COOKING MEASUREMENT EQUIVALENTS

16 tablespoons = 1 cup
12 tablespoons = 3/4 cup
10 tablespoons + 2 teaspoons = 2/3 cup
8 tablespoons = 1/2 cup
6 tablespoons = 3/8 cup
5 tablespoons + 1 teaspoon = 1/3 cup
4 tablespoons = 1/4 cup
2 tablespoons = 1/8 cup
2 tablespoons + 2 teaspoons = 1/6 cup
1 tablespoon = 1/16 cup
2 cups = 1 pint
2 pints = 1 quart
3 teaspoons = 1 tablespoon
48 teaspoons = 1 cup

STEAMPUNK RESOURCES

http://www.clockworkcabaret.com/

http://www.flickr.com/photos/7529675@N08/sets/72157603967055764/

http://reverenddr.deviantart.com/

http://onewhospinsflags.deviantart.com/

http://damnitsasha.deviantart.com/

http://vladislausdantes.deviantart.com/

http://www.myspace.com/etsysteamteam

http://www.abneypark.com/

http://en.wikipedia.org/wiki/Steampunk

http://steampunkworkshop.com/

www.datamancer.net

www.brassgoggles.co.uk

http://www.steamtreehouse.com/

http://etheremporium.pbwiki.com/

http://delen.deviantart.com/

16612182R00053

Printed in Great Britain
by Amazon